51 Easter Dessert Ideas

Scrumptious Easter Recipes For Any Occasion

By Brianne Heaton

© Revelry Publishing 2014

Copyright 2014 by Revelry Publishing

All Rights reserved under International and Pan-American Copyright Conventions. By payment of required fees, you have been granted the non-exclusive, non-transferable right to access and read the text of this book. No part of this text may be reproduced, transmitted, downloaded, decompiled, reverse-engineered or stored in or introduced into any information storage and retrieval system, in any form or by any means, whether electronic or mechanical, now known, hereinafter invented, without express written permission of the publisher.

DISCLAIMER

All information in this book has been carefully researched and checked for factual accuracy. However, the authors and publishers make no warranty, express or implied, that the information contained herein is appropriate for every individual, situation or purpose, and assume no responsibility for errors or omissions. The reader assumes the risk and full responsibility for all actions, and the authors will not be held responsible for any loss or damage, whether consequential, incidental, special or otherwise that may result from the information presented in this publication.

We have relied on our own experience as well as many different sources for this book, and we have done our best to check facts and to give credit where it is due. In the event that any material is incorrect or has been used without proper permission, please contact us so that the oversight can be corrected.

ISBN-13: 978-0993969829

ISBN-10: 0993969828

Other books by Brianne Heaton:

<u>51 Dump Cake Recipes: Scrumptious Dump Cake Desserts To Satisfy Your Sweet Tooth</u>

Baking does not have to be difficult or intimidating. You can make a delicious cake in just a few steps, with just a few ingredients by using a "dump" cake recipe. Dump cakes make less mess than traditional cakes and offer unusual and decadent choices that will wow those fortunate enough to have a bite.

<u>56 Breakfast Sandwich Recipes: Irresistible Sandwich Ideas to Kickstart Your Morning</u>

Breakfast is the most important meal of the day so it makes sense to treat it so. Are you finding it difficult to get the right balance and variety of taste experiences every day? With breakfast sandwich mania in full swing, there is no shortage of breakfast ideas here.

<u>50 Holiday Dessert Recipes: Delectable Dessert Ideas For The Christmas Holidays And Other Special Occasions</u>

Wow your family and friends with the most decadent cakes, creamiest cheesecakes, most delicious cookies, juiciest pies and most interesting international desserts! It's time to bring the baker in you to the surface and make the best desserts ever! Indulge in these holiday delights with the confidence of having made it yourself!

<u>46 Sriracha Flavored Recipes: Delicious Sriracha Hot Sauce Cookbook For A Spicy Palate</u>

Check out these delectable dessert, appetizer, entree, and drink recipes and see how Sriracha can enrich even the dullest of meals. Follow our meal plan for a whole week full of delicious Sriracha meals. Your taste buds will thank you for it.

Get the latest update on new releases from the author at:

https://www.brianneheaton.com/newsletter

Table of Contents

Introduction 1

Cakes 3

    1 - Carrot Cake Forever 5

    2 - Mom's Bunny Cake 7

    3 - Pound of Easter Lamb Cake 9

    4 - Coconut Layer Cake 11

    5 - Bunny Basket Cake 13

    6 - Easter Bunny Cake 15

    7 - Golden Pound Cake 16

    8 - Raspberry Sorbet Layer Cake 18

    9 - Very Berry Lemon Cakes 19

    10 - Pineapple Meringue Cake 21

Pies 23

    11 - Sweet Potato Pie 25

    12 - Custard Pie 27

    13 - Raspberry Chiffon Pie 29

    14 - Key Lime Pie 31

    15 - Banana Cream Pie 32

    16 - Coconut Cream Pie 33

    17 - Caramel Pecan Pie 35

18 - Peaches and Cream Pie 37

19 - Chocolate Cream Pie 39

20 - Coconut Cream Pie 41

Tarts 42

21 - Raspberry Tart 43

22 - Ricotta Raspberry Phyllo Tart 45

23 - French Apple Tart 47

24 - Country Fruit Tart 50

25 - Simple Fruit Tart 52

26 - Egg Tarts 54

27 - Blueberry Mango Cheese Tart 56

28 - Tiny Strawberry Tarts 57

29 - Mini Fudge Tarts 59

30 - Berry Butterscotch Tart 61

Pastries 63

31 - Apple Turnovers 65

32 - Mini Choco Pastry Puffs 67

33 - Danish Pastry 68

34 - Monkey Bread 70

35 - Cinnamon Rolls 71

36 - Crescent Buns with Almonds 73

37 - Jammin' Pinwheel Cookies 75

38 - Strawberry and Custard Puff Pastry Bunnies 77

39 - Meyer Lemon Pastry 79

40 - Nutella Pastry Puff 81

Children's Treats 82

41 - Nested Bunny Eggs 83

42 - Easter Bunny Cupcakes 84

43 - Nutty Buddy Easter Chicks 85

44 - Easter Peeps Cream Delight 86

45 - Easter Bunny Racers 87

46 - Bunny Bread 88

47 - Easter Egg Nests 90

48 - Choco Krispie Easter Treats 91

49 - Chocolate Creamy Easter Eggs 92

50 - Peeping S'mores 94

51 - Bunny Cups 95

Thank You 96

Other Books by Brianne Heaton 97

About the Author – Brianne Heaton 98

Connect with Brianne Heaton 99

Scrumptious Easter Recipes For Any Occasion

Introduction

It's the night before Easter. The eggs have been decorated and hidden. The sports coats and dresses for church tomorrow have been pressed and are laying out flat to avoid more wrinkles. The house is spotless and ready for your guests. Everything is ready to cook a delicious Easter dinner except one thing...

The dessert!

Luckily, we've got you covered. This collection of 51 Easter dessert recipes has something tasty and enticing for everyone, and you don't have to be Julia Child in order to pull them off.

Our list of cakes, pies, tarts and pastries is diverse. Fresh fruits like pineapple, raspberries, and strawberries will bring color and an added taste of spring to your dinner. If your family demands chocolate, we have the perfect recipes to satisfy any sweet tooth.

All of these recipes can be altered to accommodate a family member with a nut allergy. You can also modify the ingredients to fit a vegan lifestyle, but this might change the taste of the finished project.

So what are you waiting for? Go preheat the oven and get cooking!

Scrumptious Easter Recipes For Any Occasion

Cakes

Scrumptious Easter Recipes For Any Occasion

1 - Carrot Cake Forever

Makes two 10-inch (25 cm) round layers

Ingredients:

- 1 teaspoon salt
- 1½ teaspoons baking soda
- 2 teaspoons vanilla extract
- 4 teaspoons ground cinnamon
- 1 cup brown sugar
- 1 cup raisins
- 1 cup vegetable oil
- 1 cup crushed pineapple, drained
- 1¼ cups chopped walnuts
- 1½ cups white sugar
- 3 cups all-purpose flour
- 6 cups grated carrots
- 4 eggs
- Cream cheese frosting

Directions:

1. Get out a medium-sized bowl and throw in the grated carrots and brown sugar.
2. Let them sit for 60 minutes and then stir in the raisins.
3. While they're sitting, set the oven to 350°F (175°C).
4. Coat a baking pan with grease and flour it.
5. Lightly beat the eggs in a large bowl.
6. Now carefully beat in the white sugar, oil and vanilla.
7. Once they are mixed, add the pineapple.
8. In a separate bowl, measure out the flour, baking soda, salt and cinnamon.
9. Mix them together and then pour them into the wet mixture.
10. Add your carrot mix last and add one cup of the walnuts (save some walnuts for the frosting).
11. Now carefully pour the completed batter into the greased pan.
12. Bake the cake for 45 to 50 minutes until the cake passes the toothpick test.
13. Let it cool on a wire rack for ten minutes, and then remove it from the pan.
14. After the cake has cooled completely, it is ready for a cream cheese frosting or one of your choosing.
15. After frosting, sprinkle the remaining walnuts on top.

2 - Mom's Bunny Cake

Recipe makes one molded cake

Ingredients:

- ¾ teaspoon orange extract
- 1 teaspoon clear vanilla extract
- 1¼ teaspoons salt
- 1¼ teaspoons vanilla extract
- 1½ teaspoons lemon extract
- 1¾ teaspoons baking powder
- 2 tablespoons milk at room temperature
- ½ cup vegetable shortening
- ½ cup butter at room temperature
- $1\frac{1}{8}$ cups unsalted butter at room temperature
- $1\frac{1}{3}$ cups milk at room temperature
- 2 cups white sugar
- 3 cups all-purpose flour
- 4 cups confectioners' sugar
- 4 eggs at room temperature

Directions:

1. First prepare the oven. Make sure there is a rack on the lower third of the oven and it is set to 320°F (165°C).
2. Coat and flour the cake pan with vegetable shortening. Use a bunny-shaped one or try making an Easter egg.
3. In a bowl, combine the flour, baking powder and salt.
4. In another bowl, combine the milk, lemon extract, 1¼ teaspoons vanilla extract, and orange extract.
5. Using an electric mixer, beat the unsalted butter on medium speed for about two minutes.
6. Once it's creamy, add the white sugar and continue to beat them together. You will need to scrape the bowl on occasion. After about five minutes, the mix should be fluffy.
7. Now add each egg one at a time. Beat well in between eggs.
8. Now bring the speed back down to low.

9. If you have a pour attachment, attach it to the mixing bowl now.
10. Carefully add in the flour and milk mixtures. Alternate between them, starting and ending with the flour mixture.
11. Be careful not to beat the mixture too much and be sure to scrape the bowl from time to time.
12. Once all of the ingredients have been added and mixed, pour the batter into the cake pan and bake in the oven for 30 to 45 minutes until the top is a light brown color and it passes the tooth pick test.
13. Insert a toothpick into the middle of the cake. If it comes out clean, the cake is done.
14. Check often to avoid over baking it.
15. Take out the cake and set it on a wire rack.
16. Let it cool for about 15 minutes.
17. Now flip the pan over and let it fall gently out of the pan and onto the rack.
18. Let it cool entirely, about 3 or 4 hours.
19. Now for the icing. Combine the vegetable shortening, ½ cup butter, confectioner's sugar, 2 tablespoons milk, and 1 teaspoon vanilla extract in a mixing bowl and beat it, preferable with the electric mixer.
20. Once it is nice and creamy, it's done.
21. Now scoop the frosting into a plastic bag with a seal on it.
22. Move all of the frosting into one corner and clip the corner with scissors.
23. Seal the bag and frost the cake in any way you desire.
24. Serve and enjoy!

3 - Pound of Easter Lamb Cake

Makes one pound cake

Ingredients:

- 2 teaspoons vanilla
- 2 teaspoons almond extract
- $1/3$ cup bourbon
- ½ cup chopped pecans
- 1 pound (450 gm) butter, room temperature
- 2 cups white frosting
- 3 cups sugar, divided
- 3 cups sifted all-purpose flour
- 8 eggs, separated
- Sweetened flaked coconut for decorating
- Jelly beans or other small candies as desired

Directions:

1. Set the oven to 350°F (175°C).
2. Prepare the lamb-shaped cake mold by greasing it and then flouring it.
3. In a large bowl, add the butter and 2 cups of sugar and beat them together with an electric mixer.
4. Once they are fluffy-looking, add the egg yolks one at a time and beat into the mixture before adding the next.
5. Now alternate between adding the flour, vanilla, almond extract, and bourbon.
6. Mix until all ingredients have been successfully added.
7. In another bowl, add the egg whites and beat until they're foamy.
8. Gradually add the sugar and beat until medium peaks form in the batter.
9. Now raise the whisk straight up: the tip of the peak should curl ever-so slightly.
10. With a whisk or rubber spatula, carefully fold over $1/3$ of the egg white mix into the batter. This should lighten the batter.

11. Now fold over the remaining egg whites and toss in the chopped pecans.
12. Measure out about 1 cup into the cake pan.
13. Carefully place a toothpick into each ear and nose. This will help hold the ears and nose together.
14. Now pour the remaining batter into the mold and put it in the oven.
15. The cake will need to bake for about 1½ hours. It should pass the toothpick test.
16. Let the pan cool for 10 minutes before carefully removing the cake from the pan onto a wire rack.
17. Once everything has cooled, set in on a serving plate, frost it, and decorate it with the coconut and candies.

4 - Coconut Layer Cake

Makes two 9-inch (22.5 cm) layers

Ingredients:

- ¼ teaspoon cream of tartar
- ¼ teaspoon salt
- ¾ teaspoon salt
- 1 teaspoon almond extract
- 1 teaspoon vanilla extract
- 1 teaspoon vanilla extract
- 4½ teaspoons baking powder
- 2 tablespoons water
- ⅓ cup corn syrup
- ¾ cup white sugar
- 1 cup flaked coconut
- 1½ cups white sugar
- 2 cups milk
- 3 cups sifted all-purpose flour

- 3 eggs

Cake

Directions:

1. Prepare the oven and cake pans first. Set the oven to 350°F (175°C) and grease two 9-inch (22.5 cm) round pans.
2. In two bowls, separate 2 egg yolks from the whites. You'll need the whites for frosting.
3. Now in another bowl, cream the shortening and toss in 1½ cups of sugar with the beaten yolks and 1 egg white.
4. Beat them all together.
5. Now sift the flour along with the baking powder and salt.
6. Add the coconut and mix in milk and almond extract, which should be added alternatively.
7. Combine this with the shortening and then pour into the pans.
8. Let the cake bake at 350°F (175°C) for roughly 30 minutes. Check from time to time.
9. Let the cakes cool before removing them from the pans.
10. Frost the cakes with the Angel frosting and season with shredded coconut on the tops and sides of the cake.

Frosting

Directions:

1. With the remaining 2 egg whites, add ¾ cup white sugar, corn syrup, water, cream of tartar, and salt to a double boiler, which should be over hard boiling water.
2. Immediately beat with a beater until the mixture stands in stiff mounds.
3. Take the mixture off the heat and add vanilla or other flavoring.
4. Be sure to keep beating until the mixture is so thick that it can easily be spread.
5. Frost the cake and enjoy!

5 - Bunny Basket Cake

Recipe makes one 8-inch (20 cm) round basket

Ingredients:

- ½ teaspoon water
- 2 cups flaked coconut
- 1 package (14 ounce or 390 gm) candy-coated chocolate pieces
- 1 package (18.25 ounce or 500 gm) white cake mix
- 1 can (16 ounce or 450 gm) white frosting
- 2 drops green food coloring

Directions:

1. Prepare two 8-inch (20 cm) round cake pans according to the package directions.
2. Mix the cake batter as directed and bake the cake, setting the oven to the package's directions.
3. Let the cake cool completely.
4. Once cooled, cut a circle in the center of one of the cakes and remove it.
5. The ring remaining should measure about 1½ inch (3.75 cm) thick all around.
6. Set the other layer on a platter and frost the top of it.
7. Now add the ring on top of the frosted cake and continue to frost the sides and top of the cake.
8. To decorate, place the candy pieces into the frosting.
9. To make the green Easter grass, add water and green food coloring to a medium bowl.
10. Carefully add the coconut and stir with a fork until the coconut looks evenly tinted.
11. Set the coconut in the center of the basket.
12. Now for a handle. Cut a piece of aluminum foil measuring about 18 x 16 inch (45 x 40 cm).
13. Fold it lengthwise four times.
14. Wind a ribbon around it for color and secure with tape.

15. Now carefully secure this on top and fill the basket with candies.

6 - Easter Bunny Cake

Makes twelve servings

Ingredients:

- 3¾ cups flaked coconut
- 1 package (18.25 ounce or 500 gm) yellow cake mix
- 1 package (16 ounce or 450 gm) vanilla frosting
- 4 red licorice
- 30 small jellybeans

Directions:

1. Get two 9-inch (22.5 cm) round pans ready for baking by following the directions on the cake mix box and heat the oven as directed.
2. In addition to following the cake batter mix directions on the box, add a ½ cup of coconut.
3. Pour the batter evenly between the two pans and back and cool as directed.
4. Once the cake is done, let it cool.
5. When it's room temperature, set one whole cake on a serving tray to make the bunny's head.
6. Now cut part of the second cake into two convex ears.
7. Set on both sides of the head.
8. Cut another convex shape for the bow tie and place it about ½ inch (1.25 cm) below the head. Now frost the entire bunny from the top to the sides.
9. Gently pat the remaining coco nut into the sides and decorate the bunny face and bowtie using the jelly beans and licorice.

7 - Golden Pound Cake

Ingredients:

- ½ teaspoon salt
- 1 teaspoon baking powder
- 2 teaspoon vanilla extract
- ¼ cup honey
- 1 cup butter, softened
- 1 ⅓ cup sugar
- 1 ¾ cup flour, sifted
- 5 large eggs

Directions:

1. Set the oven to 325°F (165 °C).
2. Spread oil over a 6-cup loaf pan.
3. In a bowl combine the butter, sugar, and honey and beat using an electric mixer on high speed.
4. Once the mix looks fluffy and light, add the eggs one at a time.
5. Now toss in the vanilla extract followed by the flour, baking powder, and salt.

6. Beat the batter until it is smooth.
7. Carefully spoon the batter into the prepared pan and bake for about 1 hour or until the cake passes the toothpick test.
8. Let the cake cool for 15 minutes before removing it from the pan.

8 - Raspberry Sorbet Layer Cake

Ingredients:

- 3 tablespoon Chambord or other raspberry-flavored liqueur
- 3 cups Vanilla Ice Cream, slightly softened
- 4 cup Raspberry Sorbet, slightly softened
- 1 pint (500 ml) Fresh Raspberries, rinsed and picked over
- 2 Frozen Pound Cakes, crusts removed, sliced into ¼-inch (0.6 cm) thick slices

Directions:

1. For this recipe, first prepare the pan. Get out parchment paper, trace and cut out a 9 inch (22.5 cm) circle.
2. Carefully fit it into the bottom of a 9-inch (22.5 cm) springform pan.
3. Now cut out a 3 x 27-inch (7.5 x 67.5 cm) strip and carefully fit it around the sides of the pan.
4. It is best to tape the parchment in place so it doesn't move. Set this aside.
5. Now for the cake! Add a layer of pound cake to the bottom of the pan and smear the vanilla ice cream evenly over it.
6. Set this in the freezer for about 25 minutes.
7. Now add 2 cups of sorbet and top with another layer of cake.
8. Put the pan back in the freezer for another 10 minutes.
9. In a small bowl, mix the raspberries and Chambord together.
10. Once the cake has finished freezing, arrange the berries evenly onto the cake.
11. Now finish with the final layer of cake and the sorbet.
12. Wrap this pan in plastic wrap and let it sit in the freezer for 4 hours.

9 - Very Berry Lemon Cakes

Ingredients:

- ¼ teaspoon salt
- ½ teaspoon baking powder
- 1 tablespoon ginger, finely chopped
- 1 tablespoon lemon zest
- 2 tablespoon orange-flavored liqueur
- 5 tablespoon lemon juice
- 9 tablespoon butter, softened
- ⅔ cup sugar
- ¾ cup flour
- 1¼ cup fresh bread crumbs
- 2¼ cup fresh berries, such as strawberries, blueberries, and raspberries
- 1 egg
- 4 egg whites

Directions:

1. Using 1 tablespoon of butter, smear across a 6-ounce (180 ml) ramekin to prevent sticking.
2. Do this for five ramekins and set them aside.
3. Pour water into a 9 x 13-inch (22.5 x 32.5 cm) pan and place a wire rack on the bottom.
4. Set this on the stove and bring the water to a boil.
5. Once boiling, reduce the heat to medium.
6. Combine flour, bread crumbs, baking powder, and salt in a bowl and set it aside.
7. In a bowl, beat the rest of the butter with ⅓ cup of sugar together on high until the butter is light and fluffy.
8. Add the egg and the flour mixture along with 1 tablespoon of lemon juice and lemon zest.
9. Mix it all together
10. Now in a large bowl, add the egg whites and beat them on high speed.

11. Stiff peaks should form.
12. Fold the egg whites carefully into the batter then divide the batter evenly among all the ramekins.
13. Cover them tightly with aluminum foil and put them in the boiling pan.
14. Cover the pan with a lid or more aluminum foil and cook for 20 to 25 minutes.
15. Now turn off the heat and take off the lid.
16. Cover the top with a damp towel.
17. Let the ramekins cool to room temperature and take the cakes out of the ramekins.
18. In a bowl, toss in the berries, liqueur, remaining lemon juice, ¼ cup of sugar, and ginger.
19. Gently mash everything together and let it sit for about 30 minutes.
20. This will allow the berries to release their juices.
21. Now spoon the mixture over the cakes and enjoy!

10 - Pineapple Meringue Cake

Ingredients:

- $1/8$ teaspoon salt
- 2 teaspoon confectioners' sugar
- 2 teaspoons baking powder
- 3 tablespoons vanilla extract
- 5 tablespoons milk
- ½ cup unsalted butter, softened
- ¾ cup (finely chopped) pecans
- 1 cup heavy cream
- 1 cup sifted cake flour
- 1½ cup granulated sugar
- $1^2/_3$ cup crushed pineapple, drained
- 4 large eggs, separated

Directions:

1. Preheat the oven to 350°F (175°C).
2. Grease the bottoms and sides of a two 8-inch (20 cm) round cake pans using butter or cooking spray and fit two circles of parchment paper on the bottom.
3. Dust all sides with flour.
4. Now combine flour, baking powder, and salt together in a bowl and set it to the side.
5. In a separate bowl, add the butter and the white sugar and beat on medium speed with an electric mixer until the butter looks fluffy.
6. Now add the egg yolks and mix until fully combined.
7. Bring the speed down to low and add 1 teaspoon of vanilla, the flour mixture, and milk until the batter is fully blended and smooth.
8. Pour the batter evenly between the two pans and set them aside.
9. Now in a large bowl, add the egg whites and beat them on high speed until they are thick and triple in volume.

10. Add another teaspoon of vanilla and gradually pour in the rest of the white sugar.
11. Beat on high until stiff peaks form in the mixture.
12. Carefully smear this meringue over the batter and add the pecans on top.
13. Bake for about 30 to 40 minutes or until the cake passes the toothpick test.
14. Let the cakes cool completely in their pans.
15. To finish, combine heavy cream, confectioner's sugar, and the final teaspoon of vanilla together and beat until stiff peaks form.
16. Gently fold in the pineapple.
17. Flip one cake pan over, meringue side down on the serving tray.
18. Add the cream to the cake and place the second cake on top, meringue side up.
19. Set it in the refrigerator until you are ready to eat.

Pies

Scrumptious Easter Recipes For Any Occasion

11 - Sweet Potato Pie

Makes one 9-inch (22.5 cm) pie

Ingredients:

- ¼ teaspoon salt
- 1 teaspoon apple pie spice
- 2 teaspoons vanilla extract
- 3 tablespoons all-purpose flour
- ¼ cup dark corn syrup
- ½ cup butter, melted
- ¾ cup evaporated milk
- 2 cups white sugar
- 2 eggs, lightly beaten
- 2 sweet potatoes
- 1 (9-inch or 22.5 cm) unbaked deep dish pie crust

Directions:

1. Get out the pie pan and set the oven to 350°F (175°C).
2. Set the sweet potatoes in an aluminum foil-lined baking dish and put them in the oven.
3. The potatoes will be easily pierced and their skin will be loose when they're done, which should be about 30 to 45 minutes.
4. Set them aside and let them cool.
5. In a large bowl, peel and mash the cooled potatoes.
6. Add sugar, evaporated milk, butter, corn syrup, eggs, flour, vanilla extract, apple pie spice, and salt to the mashed sweet potatoes.
7. Blend the mixture with an electric mixer until the batter is fluffy.
8. Carefully pour the batter into the pie crust. Be sure to save the remaining batter for future use.
9. Let the pie bake from about 45 to 50 minutes until set and the crust is brown.

12 - Custard Pie

Makes one 9-inch (22.5 cm) pie

Ingredients:

- 1 pinch salt
- ½ teaspoon nutmeg
- 1 teaspoon vanilla extract
- 1 cup white sugar
- 2 cups milk
- 6 eggs
- 1 (9-inch or 22.5 cm) unbaked pie crust

Directions:

1. Turn on the oven and set it to 475°F (245°C).
2. Combine eggs and sugar in a large bowl and beat with an electric mixer.
3. Add in the vanilla, salt, and nutmeg and slowly stir in the milk.
4. Pour the batter into the crust.

5. Bake for 10 minutes before reducing the temperature to 350°F (175°C).
6. Let it bake for another 25 to 35 minutes until the filling has set and the crust looks browned.

13 - Raspberry Chiffon Pie

Makes one pie

Ingredients:

- ¼ teaspoon cream of tartar
- ¼ cup cold water
- ¼ cup fresh raspberries
- ⅓ cup white sugar
- ½ cup heavy whipping cream
- ⅔ cup water
- ⅔ cup white sugar
- 3 cups raspberries
- 1 package unflavored gelatin
- 1 (9-inch or 22.5 cm) prepared graham cracker crust
- 3 egg yolks, beaten
- 3 egg whites

Directions:

1. Get out a medium saucepan and combine the raspberries and ⅔ cup water.
2. Let them simmer over a low heat.
3. Once the raspberries are soft, press the mix through a sieve or strainer to get rid of the seeds and keep the pulp.
4. In a small bowl, set the gelatin and ¼ cup of cold water and place the bowl to the side so the gelatin softens.
5. Clean the sauce pan and whisk the raspberry pulp, egg yolks and ⅔ cup sugar.
6. Once whisked, set the heat to high and let the mix boil while stirring constantly.
7. Finally, remove from the heat once boiled.
8. Combine the gelatin and raspberry mixtures and stir until they have dissolved.
9. Set the pan in a cold water bath to cool completely.
10. Beat the eggs in a large mixing bowl until they're fluffy.

11. Toss in the cream of tartar and add $1/3$ cup of sugar gradually while the mixer beats constantly.
12. Whip the cream until stiff in another mixing bowl and carefully fold the cooled raspberry mixture into the meringue.
13. Carefully pour or spoon the mixture in the crust and chill it in the refrigerator for at least 2 hours.
14. Top with whole raspberries if desired.

14 - Key Lime Pie

Makes one 9-inch (22.5 cm) pie

Ingredients:

- ½ cup key lime juice
- 1 (9-inch or 22.5 cm) prepared graham cracker crust
- 1 can sweetened condensed milk
- 5 egg yolks, beaten

Directions:

1. Set the oven temperature to 375°F (190°C).
2. In a bowl, mix egg yolks, sweetened condensed milk, and lime juice together.
3. Pour the batter into the unbaked graham cracker shell.
4. Bake for 15 minutes.
5. Decorate with whipped topping and lime slices if preferred.

15 - Banana Cream Pie

Makes one 9-inch (22.5 cm) pie

Ingredients:

- ¼ teaspoon salt
- 1¼ teaspoons vanilla extract
- 2 tablespoons butter
- ⅓ cup all-purpose flour
- ¾ cup white sugar
- 2 cups milk
- 1 (9-inch or 22.5 cm) pie crust, baked
- 3 egg yolks, beaten
- 4 bananas, sliced

Directions:

1. Mix the sugar, flour and salt in a saucepan.
2. Pour in the milk and stir simultaneously.
3. Set the flame to a medium heat while you continue to stir.
4. Once the mixture begins to get bubbly, stir for another 2 minutes and then remove completely.
5. In a small bowl with the beaten egg yolks, pour in a small amount of the saucepan mixture and then quickly add the egg yolks to the saucepan mixture.
6. Cook it all together for another 2 minutes while you continue to stir.
7. Take the saucepan off the stove before adding the butter and vanilla.
8. Keep stirring until the mixture becomes smooth.
9. Cut up the bananas and place them in the pastry shell.
10. Pour the pudding mixture in the shell.
11. Place the pie in the oven and bake for 12 to 15 minutes at 350°F (175°C).
12. Take it out and let it chill for an hour.

16 - Coconut Cream Pie

Makes one 9-inch (22.5 cm) pie

Ingredients:

- ¼ teaspoon salt
- 1 teaspoon vanilla extract
- ½ cup all-purpose flour
- ¾ cup white sugar
- 1 cup frozen whipped topping, thawed
- 1 cup sweetened flaked coconut
- 3 cups half-and-half cream
- 1 (9-inch or 22.5 cm) pie shell, baked
- 2 eggs, beaten

Directions:

1. Set the oven temperature to 350°F (175°C).
2. Sprinkle the coconut over the baking sheet and let it bake for about 5 minutes.

3. Stir it occasionally so all sides are golden brown.
4. Get out a medium saucepan and add the half-and-half cream, eggs, sugar, flour, and salt.
5. Mix the ingredients well and bring to a boil over a low heat, taking care to stir constantly.
6. Take the pan off the flame and add ¾ cup of the toasted coconut and vanilla extract.
7. Keep the rest of the coconut for the garnish.
8. Spoon or pour the pie filling into the crust and chill for about 4 hours.
9. Sprinkle the remaining coconut on top.

17 - Caramel Pecan Pie

Makes one 9-inch (22.5 cm) pie

Ingredients:

- ¼ teaspoon salt
- ½ teaspoon vanilla extract
- ¼ cup butter
- ¼ cup milk
- ¾ cup white sugar
- 1 cup pecan halves
- 1 (9-inch or 22.5 cm) unbaked pie crust
- 3 eggs
- 36 individually wrapped caramels, unwrapped

Directions:

1. Set the oven to 350°F (175°C).
2. Toss the caramels, butter, and milk into a saucepan and let them cook together over low heat.

3. Stir the mix often until it is nice and smooth.
4. Turn off the heat and set aside.
5. Mix sugar, eggs, vanilla, and salt in a large bowl and slowly add the caramel mix.
6. Finally, stir in the pecans.
7. Pour or spoon the batter into the unbaked pie crust.
8. Let the pie bake for 45 to 50 minutes or until the pie is brown around the edges.
9. Take it out and let it sit until the middle has firmed.

18 - Peaches and Cream Pie

Makes one 10-inch (25 cm) pie

Ingredients:

- ½ teaspoon salt
- 1 teaspoon baking powder
- 1 teaspoon ground cinnamon
- 1 tablespoon white sugar
- 3 tablespoons butter, softened
- ½ cup milk
- ½ cup white sugar
- ¾ cup all-purpose flour
- 1 package non-instant vanilla pudding mix
- 1 egg
- 1 can sliced peaches, drained and syrup reserved
- 1 package cream cheese, softened

Directions:

1. Turn the oven on and set it to 350°F (175°C).
2. Use butter to grease the sides and bottom of a 10-inch (25 cm) deep-dish pie pan.
3. Combine flour, salt, baking powder, and pudding mix into a medium mixing bowl.
4. Add the butter, egg, and milk and mix it all together for about 2 minutes.
5. Pour the mix into a pie pan and top with peach slices on top.
6. Beat cream cheese in a small mixing bowl until it's nice and fluffy.
7. Toss in ½ cup sugar and 3 tablespoons reserved peach syrup and beat together for 2 minutes.
8. Drizzle the mixture over the peaches within 1 inch (2.5 cm) of the pan edge.
9. Finally, combine 1 tablespoon of sugar and 1 teaspoon of cinnamon to sprinkle on top.

10. Now set the whole pan in the oven and let it bake for 30 to 35 minutes until the crust is golden brown.
11. Let it chill before serving.

19 - Chocolate Cream Pie

Makes one 9-inch (22.5 cm) pie

Ingredients:

- ½ teaspoon salt
- 1½ teaspoons vanilla extract
- 1 tablespoon butter
- 3 tablespoons cornstarch
- ½ cup unsweetened cocoa powder
- 1 cup frozen whipped topping, thawed
- 1½ cups white sugar
- 3 cups milk
- 1 (9-inch or 22.5 cm) pie crust, baked
- 3 egg yolks, beaten

Directions:

1. Beat the egg yolks and sugar together in a large mixing bowl.
2. Add the cornstarch, cocoa powder, and salt.

3. Stir carefully as the milk is added.
4. In a large saucepan, cook the mixture over a medium flame, making sure to stir constantly until the mixture has successfully boiled.
5. Take the saucepan off the heat and add the butter or margarine and vanilla extract while stirring.
6. Let it cool a little, and then pour it all into the pastry shell.
7. Let it cool completely before topping it with whipped topping and serving.

20 - Coconut Cream Pie

Makes one 9-inch (22.5 cm) pie

Ingredients:

- 1½ cups milk
- 1½ cups flaked coconut
- 1 container (8-ounce or 224 gm) frozen whipped topping, thawed
- 1 (9-inch or 22.5 cm) pie shell, baked
- 1 package (5-ounce or 140 gm) instant vanilla pudding mix

Directions

1. Mix milk and pudding mix in a large bowl until it thickens.
2. Carefully fold in 1 cup of coconut and half of the frozen whipped topping.
3. Mix once more and pour into the pie crust.
4. Top the pie with the remaining whipped topping and season with the leftover coconut.
5. Let it chill in the refrigerator before serving.

Tarts

21 - Raspberry Tart

Makes one 9-inch (22.5 cm) tart

Ingredients:

- 2 tablespoons confectioners' sugar
- ½ cup butter
- 1 cup all-purpose flour
- 4 cups fresh raspberries
- 1 jar (8-ounce or 224 gm) raspberry jam

Directions

1. Mix the flour, butter and sugar together in a medium bowl until blended.
2. Let it chill for 1 hour.
3. Set the oven to 375°F (190°C) and spoon the chilled mixture into a 9 inch tart pan.
4. Let it bake for 10 minutes.
5. Take it out and let it cool.
6. Top with raspberries in the crust.

7. Microwave the jam until it boils and pour over the fruit.
8. Cover and set it in the refrigerator for 1 hour.

22 - Ricotta Raspberry Phyllo Tart

Makes six tarts

Ingredients:

- ½ teaspoon orange zest
- ½ teaspoon vanilla extract
- 1 tablespoon confectioners' sugar for dusting
- 2 tablespoons unsalted butter, melted
- ¼ cup white sugar
- 1 cup low-fat ricotta cheese
- 2 cups fresh raspberries
- 1 egg
- 1 pinch ground nutmeg
- 5 sheets phyllo dough

Directions:

1. Before starting, drain the ricotta cheese in a sieve for 20 minutes.
2. Set the oven to 350°F (175°C) and get out six 3-inch (7.5 cm) loose bottom tart pans and spray with nonfat cooking spray.
3. Keep the phyllo sheets in a stack and trace six 5-inch (12.5 cm) squares on the top sheet using a ruler (3 squares across and 2 squares down).
4. Now cut along the traced lines through all 5 stacks of dough using a very sharp knife.
5. Quickly line the tart pans with the 5 sheets of dough while brushing melted butter or margarine between the layers.
6. Trim any edges.
7. Add the ricotta, sugar, egg, orange rind, vanilla extract, and nutmeg together in a medium-sized mixing bowl and beat with an electric mixture.
8. Once the batter is smooth, pour the batter evenly in each tart pan.
9. Set the tarts in the oven and bake for 25 minutes.
10. The tarts should be lightly browned.

11. Let the tarts cool and top with raspberries.
12. Before serving, take the tarts out of the pans and sprinkle with confectioner's sugar.

23 - French Apple Tart

Makes eight servings

Pastry

Ingredients:

- 3 tablespoons cold water, or as needed
- ½ cup butter, softened
- 1⅓ cups all-purpose flour
- 1 pinch salt
- 1 egg yolk

Directions:

1. Mix 1⅓ cups of flour and salt in a bowl.
2. Toss in the butter, 1 egg yolk, and water.
3. Mix everything together until large crumbs form.
4. If the mixture appears too dry, press a handful together and stir in more water.
5. Mold the dough into a ball and wrap it tightly in plastic wrap.

6. Gently flatten it a bit and set it in the refrigerator for at least 30 minutes. This step can be done in advance, up to 3 days.

Frangipane

Ingredients:

- 1 teaspoon white sugar for decoration
- 1 tablespoon apple brandy
- 2 tablespoons all-purpose flour
- ¼ cup apricot jelly
- ½ cup butter, softened
- ½ cup white sugar
- ⅔ cup ground almonds
- 1 egg, beaten
- 1 egg yolk
- 4 medium sweet apples- peeled, cored and thinly sliced

Directions:

1. Mix the butter and ½ cup of sugar together until they are soft and fluffy.
2. Add in each egg one at a time, beating in between.
3. Carefully add the apple brandy while stirring.
4. Stir in 2 tablespoons of flour in with the ground almonds and mix it all together into the batter.

Tart

Directions:

1. Take out the dough and roll it out in a 12-inch (30 cm) circle on a floured surface.
2. Fold any loose quarters in and center the point in a pie or 10-inch (25 cm) tart pan.
3. Now unfold the dough and carefully press it into the bottoms and sides.
4. Be sure to prick with a fork and gently fluke the edges.
5. Put the pastry back in the refrigerator and let it chill until it is firm.

6. Turn the oven to 400°F (200°C), and set a baking sheet inside the oven while it heats up.
7. Smear the frangipane into the pastry, which should be chilled by now. Make sure the layer is even.
8. Top with the apple slices artfully arranged in an overlapping spiral pattern.
9. One side of each piece of apple should be pressing into the frangipane until the edges touch the pastry base and overlap the previous slice.
10. To make it easier, start on the outside and work towards the center.
11. Now that the baking sheet is nice and warm, set the pie plate on the sheet in the oven.
12. Let the pie bake for 15 minutes or until the pie filling looks brown.
13. Bring the temperature down to 350°F (175°C).
14. Let the pie bake for another 10 minutes, then season with sugar over the top of the tart.
15. Set the pie back in the oven for a final 10 minutes.
16. The sugar should begin to caramelize.
17. Take the tart out and let it cool on the wire rack.
18. Just before you are about to serve, warm up the apricot jelly.
19. If the jam needs to be more of a liquid consistency, add water.
20. Brush the jelly onto the tart and serve.

24 - Country Fruit Tart

Makes one 8-inch (20 cm) tart

Ingredients:

- ¼ teaspoon ground nutmeg
- ¼ teaspoon ground cardamom
- ½ teaspoon ground cinnamon
- 1½ tablespoons cornstarch
- 1 pear- peeled, cored and sliced
- ¼ cup orange juice
- ⅓ cup brown sugar
- ½ cup apricot jam, warmed
- ½ cup butter, chilled
- ½ cup cream cheese
- 1½ cups all-purpose flour
- 2 apples- peeled, cored, and thinly sliced

Directions:

1. Using a knife or pastry blender, slice the cold butter and cream cheese into the flour.
2. The mixture should look like coarse crumbs.
3. If you prefer, use a food processor and pulse until the mixture looks like cornmeal, then add the cream cheese and pulse it until it looks like small peas.
4. The mixture should now easily form a ball.
5. Shape the dough into a rounded disk shape and wrap it up in plastic.
6. Let it refrigerate for at least 1 hour.
7. Add the apple slices and pears in the orange juice.
8. Combine the brown sugar, cinnamon, nutmeg, cardamom, and cornstarch and whisk together.
9. Add the fruit to the mixture and set aside.
10. Set the oven temperature to 375°F (190°C).
11. Get out an 8-inch (20 cm) tart pan.

12. If you plan to make a free-form tart (galette), then grease a baking sheet before starting.
13. Get out the pastry and set it on a lightly floured surface, making a 10-inch (25 cm) circle.
14. Put the dough on the tart pan or baking sheet.
15. Arrange the fruit however desired in the pastry.
16. For the baking sheet tart, leave a 2-inch (5 cm) rim of dough. If needed, fold up the edges over the fruit.
17. Put the tart in the oven and bake for about 30 minutes.
18. The filling should be bubbling.
19. Take the tart out and lightly brush it with apricot jam.

25 - Simple Fruit Tart

Makes six servings

Ingredients:

- ½ teaspoon salt
- 2 tablespoons cornstarch
- 3 tablespoons sugar
- ½ cup cold water
- 1 cup shortening
- 1 cup fresh blackberries
- 2 cups all-purpose flour
- 2 cups sliced fresh peaches

Directions:

1. Turn on the oven and set it to 450°F (230°C).
2. Combine the flour and salt in a medium bowl.
3. Now add the shortening to the mix by cutting it and then rubbing it between your fingers to create crumbles.
4. The mixture should look like oatmeal when it's done.
5. Pour in the water slowly and stir to make the dough hold together.
6. Knead the dough so that it holds together without falling apart.
7. Put it in the refrigerator while you get going on the fruit.
8. Get out another medium bowl and mix the sugar and cornstarch together.
9. Toss in the peaches and blackberries and mix it all together until the fruit is coated.
10. Put the bowl to the side.
11. Take the dough out and roll it to form a circle.
12. It should be about the size of a dinner plate.
13. Set it on a flat baking sheet.
14. Spoon the fruit mixture onto the center of the dough.
15. There should be about 1 to 2 inches (2.5 to 5 cm) of dough left around the edges.
16. Do not use any fruit juices leftover in the bowl.

17. Gently fold over the dough so some of the dough covers the fruit. It should not reach the center.
18. Place the baking sheet in the oven and let it bake for 25 to 30 minutes.
19. Once the crust reaches a light golden brown and the fruit begins to bubble, the tart is ready to come out.
20. Set it out to cool entirely.
21. Cut into wedges before serving

26 - Egg Tarts

Makes twenty-two 3-inch (7.5 cm) tarts

Ingredients:

- ¼ teaspoon vanilla extract
- 2 tablespoons cold water
- ¼ cup confectioners' sugar
- ⅜ cup evaporated milk
- 10 tablespoons butter, diced
- ¾ cup white sugar
- 1 cup water
- 2 cups all-purpose flour
- 1 pinch salt
- 1 egg
- 3 eggs

Directions:

1. Turn on the oven and set it to 400°F (200°C).
2. Combine flour and salt in a bowl.

3. Carefully add butter and blend with a pastry cutter.
4. The mixture should look like coarse crumbs.
5. In a separate bowl, combine eggs with cold water and beat together.
6. Now add the egg mixture to the flour, which should create a soft dough.
7. Wrap this up in plastic and let it refrigerate for 30 minutes.
8. Cut the dough in half and roll out each individual half to about $1/8$-inch (0.3 cm) thickness.
9. With a 3.5-inch (8.7 cm) fluted round cookie cutter, gently cut out 22 rounds.
10. Press these rounds into the 3-inch (7.5 cm) pans, which have been greased.
11. Now stir water and sugar in a saucepan over a low flame until the sugar dissolves.
12. Measure out this syrup into 1 cup and 2 tablespoons and set it aside to cool off.
13. Beat the eggs, evaporated milk, and vanilla until the mix is smooth.
14. Carefully strain the mixture into the syrup and mix it all together.
15. Now add the batter to the tart shells.
16. Let them bake for 20 minutes until the filling is set and the pastry is a light brown.

27 - Blueberry Mango Cheese Tart

Makes one 8-inch (20 cm) tart

Ingredients:

- ½ tablespoon butter
- 2 tablespoons lemon juice
- 2 tablespoons water
- $1/3$ cup confectioners' sugar for dusting
- ½ cup white sugar
- ½ cup confectioners' sugar
- 1½ cups all-purpose flour
- 2 cups blueberries
- 1 package (8 ounces or 226 gm) cream cheese, softened
- 2 mangos, peeled, seeded and chopped
- 2 egg yolks

Directions:

1. Set the oven to 350°F (175°C).
2. In a bowl, combine flour and ½ cup confectioner's sugar.
3. Cut in the butter until the mix looks like coarse crumbs.
4. Carefully mix in the egg yolks with enough water to form a ball-like shape.
5. On a floured surface, knead the dough until it is smooth and roll it out to line an 8-inch (20 cm) flan ring. You can also use a tart shell if you prefer.
6. Bake the crust for 20 minutes.
7. The pastry should be a golden brown.
8. Let it cool.
9. Add ½ cup sugar, cheese, mangos, and lemon juice to a bowl.
10. Beat with an electric mixture until the batter looks smooth.
11. There should still be a few chunks of mangos.
12. Spoon into the pastry shell and add blueberries to the top.
13. Sprinkle confectioner's sugar if needed.

28 - Tiny Strawberry Tarts

Makes seventy tarts

Ingredients:

- 3 drops red food coloring
- ¼ cup cornstarch
- ¼ cup water
- 1½ cups whipped topping (optional)
- 1 cup white sugar
- 2 cups butter
- 3½ cups boiling water
- 4½ cups all-purpose flour
- 2 packages (8 ounce or 226 gm each) cream cheese, softened
- 3 packages (3 ounce or 85 gm each) strawberry flavored Jell-O® mix
- 3 pounds (1.35 kg) fresh strawberries, sliced

Directions:

1. Set the oven to 350°F (175°C).
2. Use cooking spray to grease the muffin pans.
3. In a large bowl, combine the cream cheese and butter together with an electric mixer.
4. Once the mix is smooth, add the flour one cup at a time, beating constantly.
5. After the dough is fully mixed, roll out the dough and make 70 small dough balls.
6. Gently press the balls into the mini muffin pan cup.
7. This will form the pastry crust.
8. Place the pans in the oven and let them bake until the edges are golden brown, which should take between 15 and 18 minutes.
9. Once done, let them cool.
10. In the boiling water, add the gelatin, sugar and food coloring and stir it up.
11. Turn the heat to high and let it boil once more.
12. As it boils, add the cornstarch and water, which should turn the mixture into a paste consistency.
13. Once the gelatin dissolves completely, turn off the flame and let the mixture cool entirely.
14. This will take approximately 30 minutes.
15. Once cool, carefully spoon the gelatin paste into the baked shells.
16. Cut the strawberries in half and push one half into each tart.
17. Add a dollop of whipped topping before serving.

29 - Mini Fudge Tarts

Makes thirty tarts

Ingredients:

- ¼ teaspoon salt
- 1 teaspoon vanilla extract
- 1 teaspoon vanilla extract
- 3 tablespoons water
- ¼ cup butter, softened
- ¼ cup unsweetened cocoa powder
- ½ cup butter, softened
- ½ cup white sugar
- ½ cup flaked coconut
- 1½ cups all-purpose flour
- 1 egg yolk

Directions:

1. Turn on the oven and set it to 350 °F (175 °C).
2. Combine flour and salt in a medium sized bowl and stir.
3. Use a pastry cutter or fork to cut in butter so that only small lumps remain in the mixture.
4. Carefully sprinkle in the water along with 1 teaspoon of vanilla
5. Mix well using a fork.
6. Set the bowl aside for now.
7. Get out another bowl and add ¼ cup butter, egg yolk and sugar and mix until the batter is smooth.
8. Add 1 teaspoon vanilla and beat.
9. Now add cocoa and coconut milk.
10. Mix until everything looks smooth.
11. Set this bowl off to the side.
12. Get out a cloth-covered board and dust it with sugar.
13. Using half the dough at a time, roll it out on the sugar coated board to about a $1/16$-inch (1.5 mm) thickness.
14. Gently slice the dough into 2½-inch (6.2 cm) squares.
15. Smear 1 teaspoon of the filling onto the squares.

16. Carefully lift up the corners to the center of the pastry and seal by pressing on it.
17. Set the squares on a greased cooking sheet so that they are 2 inches (5 cm) apart.
18. Set the cookie sheet in the oven and bake for 15 to 20 minutes.
19. Once the edges are golden brown, take them out and let them cool on the sheet.
20. Move them to a wire rack to cool entirely.
21. Serve and enjoy!

30 - Berry Butterscotch Tart

Makes eight servings

Ingredients:

- ¼ teaspoon salt
- ½ teaspoon almond extract
- 1 teaspoon vanilla extract
- 2 tablespoons slivered almonds, toasted
- 2 tablespoons Smucker's® Seedless Red Raspberry Jam
- 2 tablespoons Smucker's® Butterscotch Spoonable Ice Cream Topping
- ⅓ cup sugar
- 6 tablespoons CRISCO® Butter Shortening, chilled
- ½ cup slivered almonds, toasted, plus
- ½ cup Smucker's® Seedless Red-Raspberry Jam
- ½ cup Smucker's® Butterscotch Spoonable Ice Cream Topping
- 1 cup Pillsbury BEST® All Purpose Flour
- 5 cups fresh berry mix of blackberries, blueberries, raspberries and strawberries (large berries to be quartered)
- 1 large egg

Directions:

1. Set the oven to 350°F (175°C).
2. In a processor or blender, add flour, salt, and sugar and mix them for 10 seconds.
3. Toss in shortening and let it blend again until the mixture looks like coarse crumbs.
4. Now crack in the eggs and spoon in the vanilla and almond extract.
5. Keep mixing until moist clumps form.
6. Be sure to scrape the side of the blender with a rubber spatula from time to time.
7. Take the dough out of the blender and roll it into a ball. Coat your fingers in flour to make this easier.

8. Shape the dough onto the bottom and sides of a 9-inch (22.5 cm) tart pan. Use one with a removable bottom.
9. Pour ½ cup of almonds over the bottom of the crust and smear a ½ cup of jam over those almonds.
10. On top of the jam, add a ½ cup of butterscotch topping and smear it over the jam.
11. Put the tart in the oven and bake for about 40 minutes.
12. The crust edges will be golden, and the jam will look thick and will bubble slightly.
13. Take out the pan and let it cool completely before pushing up on the pan bottom to get the tart out.
14. In a bowl, combine the berries with 2 tablespoons of jam.
15. Spread this on the tart and add the remaining almonds to the edges of the tart.
16. Drizzle the last of the butterscotch over the tart.

Pastries

Scrumptious Easter Recipes For Any Occasion

31 - Apple Turnovers

Makes 8 turnovers

Ingredients:

- 1 teaspoon vanilla extract
- 1 teaspoon ground cinnamon
- 1 tablespoon cornstarch
- 1 tablespoon water
- 1 tablespoon milk
- 2 tablespoons lemon juice
- 2 tablespoons butter
- 1 cup brown sugar
- 1 cup confectioners' sugar
- 4 cups water
- 1 package (17.25 ounce or 483 gm) frozen puff pastry sheets, thawed
- 4 Granny Smith apples- peeled, cored and sliced

Directions

1. Get out a large bowl and add the lemon juice and 4 cups of water.
2. Drop in the apple slices to stop them from browning.
3. Set a large skillet over a medium flame and melt the butter.
4. Take the apples out of the water, drain, and add them to the skillet.
5. After about 2 minutes, toss in brown sugar and cinnamon.
6. Let it all cook for 2 more minutes. Be sure to keep stirring.
7. Add in cornstarch and 1 tablespoon of water.
8. Let everything cook together until the sauce looks nice and thick.
9. Take off the heat and let it cool a little.
10. Turn on the oven and set it to 400 °F (200 °C).
11. Take out the puff pastries and check for cracks.
12. Push the dough together to hide any cracks you find.
13. Cut each sheet into a neat square and then cut each square into 4 smaller squares.
14. Spoon out the apple mixture into the center of each square.
15. Now carefully fold the corners over so you have a triangle shape.
16. Press on the edges to seal the pastry.
17. Set all the squares on a baking sheet, keeping them about 1 inch (2.5 cm) apart.
18. Let them bake for about 25 minutes.
19. Once the pastry shells look browned and puffed up, take them out and let them cool completely before pouring glaze over them.
20. Combine confectioner's sugar, milk and vanilla together to make the glaze. You may have to add more sugar to make the icing thicker.
21. Spoon over the pastries and serve.

32 - Mini Choco Pastry Puffs

Makes thirty puffs

Ingredients:

- 3 tablespoon sugar
- $\frac{1}{3}$ cup unsweetened cocoa powder
- 1 cup heavy cream
- ½ of a 17.3-ounce (490 gm) package Pepperidge Farm® Puff Pastry Sheets (1 sheet), thawed
- Unsweetened baking cocoa, chocolate curls or chocolate sprinkles (optional)

Directions:

1. Turn on the oven and set it to 400°F (200°C).
2. Sprinkle flour over a large surface and spread out the pastry.
3. With flour on your fingertips, shape the pastry into a 14 x 9-inch (35 x 22.5 cm) rectangle.
4. Now cut up the pastry into 30 rounds.
5. You will use a 1¾-inch (4.4 cm) cookie or biscuit cutter for this step.
6. Set the pastry rounds on a baking sheet approximately 2 inches (5 cm) apart from each other.
7. Use a fork to prick them and brush water on them.
8. Add 1½ teaspoons of sugar on top.
9. Put the baking sheet in the oven and let it bake for 10 minutes.
10. Once they look golden brown, take them out of the oven and let them cool on a wire rack for about 10 minutes.
11. In a medium bowl, use an electric mixer to mix cream, cocoa and the remaining sugar. Stiff peaks should form.
12. Slice the pastries in half into 2 layers.
13. From the chocolate mixture, spoon out 2 teaspoons onto all 30 bottoms.
14. Place the top half of pastry back on and sprinkle cocoa powder on top.

33 - Danish Pastry

Makes thirty-six pastries

Ingredients:

- 1 teaspoon lemon extract
- 1 teaspoon almond extract
- 2 teaspoons salt
- 4½ teaspoons active dry yeast
- ½ cup white sugar
- ⅔ cup all-purpose flour
- 2 cups unsalted butter, softened
- 2½ cups milk
- 8 cups all-purpose flour
- 2 eggs
- 6 ounce (180 ml) fruit preserves for filling (your choice)

Directions:

1. Beat the butter and ⅔ cup of flour in a medium sized bowl.
2. Cut the dough in half and roll out the two halves between two pieces of waxed paper and place them in a 6 x 12-inch (15 x 30 cm) sheet.
3. Put it in the refrigerator.
4. Combine dry yeast and 3 cups of flour in a large mixing bowl.
5. Set it aside.
6. In a medium saucepan, mix the milk, sugar, and salt over medium heat.
7. Bring it up to 115°F (45°C) so it's warm but not hot.
8. Once done, add the milk mix to the flour and throw in the eggs and lemon and almond extracts.
9. Mix everything together for 3 minutes.
10. Now carefully knead in the last ½ cup of flour a little at a time so the dough is now firm.
11. Set this aside to sit until it doubles in size.
12. Once doubled, cut the dough in half.
13. With each half of the dough, roll them out to make 14-inch (35 m) squares.

14. Set one sheet of the cold butter onto a piece of the dough and fold the dough so it resembles a book cover.
15. Use your fingers to seal the edges.
16. Now roll the pieces out to a 20 x 12-inch (50 x 30 cm) rectangle.
17. Now fold it into thirds. To do this, fold the long sides in over to the center. Keep doing this and roll it into a large rectangle and folding it into thirds.
18. Use plastic wrap to wrap it completely and set it in the refrigerator for 30 minutes.
19. After 30 minutes, take the dough out of the refrigerator one at a time and repeat the rolling and folding process two more times.
20. Put it back in the fridge to chill once more. Be warned that warm butter will make the dough hard to handle.
21. To create the Danish pastries, take the dough out and roll it to ¼-inch (0.6 cm) thickness.
22. Cut it into squares and place the filling in the center.
23. Fold over two of the corners over the filling to create a diamond shape. You can also fold the dough in half and cut it into 1-inch strips. Stretch the strips, twist, and roll it into a neat spiral. Spoon some of the preserves or other filling into the center.
24. Once the Danish pastries are rolled, set them on a baking sheet. You do not need to grease it.
25. Let the dough rise to twice its original size.
26. Set the oven temperature to 450°F (230°C).
27. Brush the Danish pastries with egg white to create a shiny finish.
28. Bake the Danish pastries for about 8 to 10 minutes.
29. Once the crust turns a light golden brown, it's done.

34 - Monkey Bread

Makes one using a 10-inch (25 cm) tube pan

Ingredients:

- 2 teaspoons ground cinnamon
- ½ cup chopped walnuts (optional)
- ½ cup raisins
- ½ cup margarine
- 1 cup white sugar
- 1 cup packed brown sugar
- 3 packages (12 ounce or 336 gm each) refrigerated biscuit dough

Directions:

1. Set the oven to 350 °F (175 °C).
2. Get out a Bundt® pan or one 9-10-inch (22.5 to 25 cm) tube pan and grease it.
3. In a plastic bag, combine white sugar and cinnamon.
4. Slice the biscuits into quarters and put 6 to 8 of the quarters into the plastic bag.
5. Shake it with the sugar and cinnamon mix.
6. Set the pieces on the greased pan and repeat the process until all of the biscuits have been coated in sugar and cinnamon.
7. Sprinkle in nuts and raisins if you desire.
8. Melt the margarine and add the brown sugar together in a small saucepan.
9. Let the mixture boil for a minute then pour it over the prepared biscuits.
10. Bake the pan for 35 minutes, then remove it and let it cool on a wire rack.
11. Once cool, flip it over onto a pan and serve.
12. You do not need to cut it, just pull it apart.

35 - Cinnamon Rolls

Makes sixteen rolls

Ingredients:

- ¾ teaspoon salt
- 1 tablespoon ground cinnamon
- ¼ cup white sugar
- ¼ cup butter, softened
- ½ cup brown sugar
- ¾ cup warm water (110°F/43°C)
- 2½ cups bread flour
- 1 package (0.25 ounce or 7 gm) active dry yeast
- 1 egg, room temperature

Directions:

1. Pour the yeast into warm water and let it dissolve in a small bowl. After sitting for 10 minutes, the mixture should be creamy.

2. Add the yeast mixture to a bowl with sugar, salt, egg, and 1 cup of flour.
3. Mix everything together so it's nicely blended, then add the last of the flour, ½ cup at a time. Be sure to beat the mixture well after adding each addition of flour.
4. Once the dough has formed, set it on a floured surface and begin to knead it. You will need it to be smooth and almost elastic-like, which should take about 8 minutes.
5. Set it in a bowl and cover it with a damp cloth for 10 minutes.
6. Spray or butter an 8 x 8-inch (20 x 20 cm) square baking pan.
7. Place the dough back on the floured surface and make a rectangle with a thickness of ¼-inch (0.6 cm).
8. Spread butter on top and season with brown sugar and cinnamon.
9. Roll the dough along the edges so they form a roll.
10. Cut the roll into 16 equally-sized pieces and put them in the baking pan. The cut side should be facing up.
11. Wrap the pan with plastic wrap and let it sit in the refrigerator overnight.
12. Take it out and let it sit at room temperature. This will cause the dough to rise to twice its original size. After about 45 minutes, it should be done.
13. Turn the oven to 400°F (200°C) and put the pan inside.
14. Bake it for 20 minutes until the sides are golden brown.

36 - Crescent Buns with Almonds

Makes twelve buns

Ingredients:

- $3/8$ teaspoon almond extract
- 2 teaspoons all-purpose flour
- 2 tablespoons milk
- 2 tablespoons butter, melted
- ¼ cup chopped toasted almonds
- ¼ cup margarine, softened
- ½ cup packed brown sugar
- ½ cup confectioners' sugar
- 2 cans (8 ounce or 226 gm each) refrigerated crescent rolls

Directions:

1. First turn on the oven and set it to 375°F (190°C).
2. In a bowl, mix softened butter or margarine, brown sugar, flour, 1 tablespoon milk, and $1/8$ teaspoon almond extract.
3. Beat everything together until it is properly mixed.
4. Carefully pour the batter into 12 spots in ungreased muffin tin.
5. Separate the crescent roll dough to make 4 long rectangles and press the perforations to seal them. Be sure to do this firmly.
6. Add some of the melted butter to $1/8$ teaspoon of almond extract and use a brush to coat the dough.
7. Sprinkle the almonds across the dough and then begin to roll it up like a jellyroll.
8. Each of the 4 rolls should then be cut into 3 equal pieces.
9. Set these pieces in the muffin cups.
10. Get out a baking sheet and put the muffin pan on it.
11. Slide the whole sheet into the oven and bake for 15 to 20 minutes.
12. Once it looks a shade of golden brown, take it out and invert the rolls right away onto a cooling rack.
13. Mix confectioners' sugar, 1 tablespoon milk, and $1/8$ teaspoon almond extract together in a bowl.

14. Spoon this over the rolls while they're warm.

37 - Jammin' Pinwheel Cookies

Makes forty pieces

Ingredients:

- ½ cup sugar
- ½ cup assorted jams (kiwi, apricot and raspberry)
- 1 package (17¼ ounce or 490 gm) frozen puff pastry (2 sheets), thawed
- 1 egg, beaten to blend (glaze)
- Powdered sugar (optional)

Directions:

1. Get the oven heated to 400°F (200 °C).
2. Set out 2 large baking sheets and lightly coat them with butter.
3. Roll out 1 puff pastry sheet on a lightly floured surface to shape a 16 x 13-inch (40 x 32.5 cm) rectangle.
4. Use a knife to trim the edges, making it a 15 x 12-inch (37.5 x 30 cm) rectangle.
5. Now slice the rectangle into twenty 3-inch (7.5 cm) squares.
6. Carefully make 1-inch-long (2.5 cm) diagonal cuts on all 4 corners of the squares.
7. The cuts should be angled toward the center, but be careful not to cut through to the center.
8. Make the pinwheels by folding every other point of the puff pastry towards the center of the square.
9. Use your thumb to carefully press the folds down and set them in place.
10. Brush egg glaze over the pinwheels and sprinkle ½ teaspoon of sugar over all the pinwheels to sweeten them.
11. At the center of each one, spoon ½ teaspoon of jam and move the pinwheels to a baking sheet.
12. It should only take about 13 minutes for them to bake.
13. They are done when they look puffed and golden brown.
14. Scoop them onto a wire rack with a metal spatula to cool.
15. Repeat the process with the remaining puff pastry sheet.

16. Sift powdered sugar on top if you like.
17. Stack the cookies with wax paper in between and store in airtight containers.
18. These can be frozen for up to 2 weeks. Let them thaw before eating. They can also be stored in airtight containers at room temperature.

38 - Strawberry and Custard Puff Pastry Bunnies

Ingredients:

- ¼ teaspoon vanilla
- 1 teaspoon grated lemon peel
- 1-2 tablespoons chunky sugar or sugar crystals
- ¼ cup white sugar
- ⅓ cup sugar
- ½ cup Marsala wine
- ½ pound (225 gm) puff pastry sheets (Pepperidge Farm Puff Pastry Sheets will do)
- 1 quart (1 L) strawberries
- 1 pint (500 ml) whipping cream, whipped
- 1 egg, beaten
- 6 egg yolks
- Garnish of mint, basil or rosemary
- Sabayon Sauce

Directions:

1. Set the oven to 400°F (200°C).
2. Take out the pastry puff sheets and let them thaw according to the directions on the package.
3. Spread flour on a large surface and unfold the pastry.
4. Use a bunny-shaped cookie cutter to cut out little bunnies.
5. Brush them with egg to make them shiny and sprinkle a bit of sugar on top.
6. Line parchment on a baking sheet or use a Silpat baking mat to bake the pastry for 15 minutes to a golden color.
7. Take them out of the oven and set them on a cooling rack.
8. Cut up the strawberries and toss them in a bowl with white sugar.
9. Let them sit for 20 to 30 minutes. This will allow them to macerate.

10. While they're sitting, mix whipped cream with an electric mixer. Set it to the side.
11. In another bowl, combine the eggs, sugar, Marsala wine, vanilla, and lemon peel.
12. Get out a saucepan, fill it halfway with water, and bring it to a simmer.
13. Lower the temperature and place the egg mixture bowl over the water. Don't let the bottom of the bowl touch the water.
14. Now whisk the contents of the bowl for 7 to 10 minutes straight. It will turn to a custard-like sauce.
15. Once it has achieved this, turn off the heat and set the bowl aside.
16. Before serving, cut the bunnies into top and bottom halves and spoon the sabayon custard, strawberries and whip cream on the bottom.
17. Place the top half of the bunny on top or serve it on the side.

39 - Meyer Lemon Pastry

Ingredients:

- 1 cup granulated sugar
- 1 cup cold heavy cream
- 2 cups water
- ½ vanilla bean, split and scraped, pod reserved for another use
- 1 package (14 ounces or 390 gm) frozen puff pastry preferably Dufour, thawed
- 1 large egg, lightly beaten, for egg wash
- 6 Meyer lemons, thinly sliced
- All-purpose flour, for surface
- Fine sanding sugar, for sprinkling

Directions:

1. In a medium saucepan, let the sugar and water simmer over medium heat.
2. Let the mix cook until the sugar dissolves, which should take about 5 minutes.
3. Get out some parchment paper and cut a circle roughly the size of the saucepan.
4. Put the lemons in the saucepan and place the parchment over it.
5. The lemons must simmer for about one and a half hours or until they look soft and slightly translucent.
6. Take the lemons out of the syrup and let them drip dry on a wire rack.
7. Turn the oven to 400 °F (200 °C).
8. Flour a surface and roll out the puff pastry to form an 11 x 14-inch (27.5 x 35 cm) rectangle.
9. Using a paring knife, score a 1-inch (2.5 cm) border around the edges.
10. Use a brush to spread the egg wash over the entire surface of the dough and season with sugar.
11. Put the pastry in the freezer for 30 minutes or until firm.
12. Now bake the pastry for 22 to 24 minutes.

13. Once the pastry is a golden brown, take it out and let it cool completely.
14. While the pastry is cooking, combine heavy cream with the vanilla seeds and whisk with an electric mixer. When soft peaks form, the mixture is done.
15. Slice the lemons if needed and arrange them on top. Serve alongside the vanilla cream.

40 - Nutella Pastry Puff

Ingredients:

- 1 tablespoon sugar for sanding the crust
- 4 tablespoons whole hazelnuts, toasted and chopped
- 7 ounces (210 ml) Nutella (roughly half of a 13-ounce jar)
- 1 sheet (from a 17.3 ounce or 490 gm package) frozen puff pastry, thawed
- 1 large egg, beaten for an egg wash
- Fleur de sel (or fine sea salt) for finishing

Directions:

1. Turn on the oven and set it to 450°F (230°C).
2. Line a baking sheet with parchment paper and set out the puff pastry.
3. Make a 10-inch (25 cm) square and fold the sides in to make a crust.
4. Use a fork to poke the middle of the dough and brush the sides with egg wash to help them cook.
5. Sprinkle sugar on the sides as well.
6. Put it in the freezer for 15 minutes.
7. Move the baking sheet to the oven and bake for 15 to 20 minutes or until the pastry looks puffy and golden brown.
8. Take it out of the oven and smear Nutella evenly over the pastry.
9. As the Nutella melts, season with sea salt and hazelnuts on top.
10. Cut the finished pastry into 4 squares or 6 triangles and serve warm.

Scrumptious Easter Recipes For Any Occasion

Children's Treats

41 - Nested Bunny Eggs

Ingredients:

- ½ cup light corn syrup
- ½ cup sugar
- ¾ cup peanut butter
- 4 cups chow mein noodles
- 36 jelly beans

Directions:

1. Using a rolling pin or other utensil, break up the noodles into smaller pieces and set them to the side in a bowl.
2. In a large saucepan, cook the sugar and corn syrup on medium heat.
3. Once done, the sugar should be melted and there will be bubbles at the sides of the pan.
4. Toss in the peanut butter and continue to stir until the mixture is smooth.
5. Pour everything into the bowl with the crushed noodles and mix until they're coated.
6. Let the mixture cool for a bit.
7. Now butter your hands and divide the mixture into roughly ¼ cup size portions.
8. Mold each portion into a compact ball and indent the middle to look like a nest.
9. Set wax paper out and place the newly formed nests on it.
10. Add the jelly beans for decorations.

42 - Easter Bunny Cupcakes

Ingredients:

- ½ teaspoon vanilla extract
- 1 cup milk
- 1 box (18¼ ounce or 510 gm) white cake mix, (as well as the other ingredients listed on the cake box to prepare the cake)
- 3 cups Betty Crocker fluffy white frosting mix
- 6 marshmallows
- Any desired food coloring
- Pink sugar
- Miniature M&M baking bits
- Chocolate sprinkles

Directions:

1. Turn on the oven to 350°F (175°C).
2. Get out 2 muffin tins (or whatever is needed to make 24) and line the tins with paper liners.
3. Follow the directions on the cake mix box, but instead of using water, use milk, and add vanilla extract.
4. Bake and cool to the specifications directed on the box.
5. Measure out 2 cups of frosting and set it in a bowl.
6. Add yellow, light blue, pale green or pink food coloring.
7. You can separate the frosting into different bowls for different colors.
8. To make the bunny face, add a dollop of white frosting to the middle of the cupcake.
9. You can pipe the frosting through a plastic bag with a seal if that's easier.
10. For the ears, slice the marshmallows in half crosswise with a sharp pair of kitchen shears then cut the individual pieces again in half diagonally, flattening gently with your fingers. Decorate with a little bit of pink sugar. Press the ears into frosting mounds to help them stick.
11. Now decorate the cupcakes using frosting, candies, and chocolate sprinkles for whiskers.

43 - Nutty Buddy Easter Chicks

Ingredients:

- Wax paper
- Black decorating gel (eyes) or icing (eyes)
- 8 orange Tic Tac mints (beak)
- 12 ounces yellow candy melts or 12 ounces white chocolate candy melts, with yellow food coloring (must be an oil-based coloring)
- 16 Nutter Butter sandwich cookies

Directions:

1. Slice the Tic Tacs in half to make the chick's beak.
2. Set them off to the side.
3. Now melt the candy according to the directions on the package. For white candies, add yellow food coloring.
4. Using a fork or spoon, carefully dip the Nutter Butter cookies into the melted candies.
5. Give the cookies a light shake to get off the excess candy.
6. Set it on the wax paper and let it harden, which should take between 10 and 20 minutes.
7. Use the decorating gel to make eyes and other designs on the chicks.
8. Add a bit of melted candy to the end of the Tic Tac to attach it to the body.

44 - Easter Peeps Cream Delight

Ingredients:

- 1 teaspoon grated Meyer lemon rind
- ½ cup Meyer lemon juice
- ½ cup whipping cream (to garnish)
- ⅔ cup sugar
- 1¼ cups heavy cream
- 1 whole egg
- 4 egg yolks
- Marshmallow peep, for decoration

Directions:

1. Set the oven to 325°F (165°C).
2. In a bowl, use a whisk to combine lemon juice, sugar, egg, and egg yolks.
3. Add cream and continue to whisk until all the sugar has dissolved.
4. Pour the mixture through a strainer and mix in the lemon rind.
5. In a large roasting pan, put in six ¾ cup pot de crème cups, or custard cups.
6. Pour the mixture evenly into the 6 cups.
7. Add hot water to the roasting pan so that it comes up to half the height of the custard cups.
8. Place aluminum foil over the pan and let it bake for about 35 minutes.
9. The custard will be set around the edges.
10. Take the pan out of the oven and set the custard cups on a wire rack to cool.
11. Once cooled, cover once more and put them in the refrigerator for 2 hours. You can leave them overnight if preferred.
12. Use an electric mixer to beat the rest of the whipping cream.
13. Once soft peaks begin to form, spoon out 1 tablespoon of the whipped cream on each pot and set a peep in the middle.

45 - Easter Bunny Racers

Ingredients:

- 1 container (16 ounce or 450 gm) vanilla frosting or 1 container (16 ounce or 450 gm) chocolate frosting
- 1 package (4½ ounce or 115 gm) peach ring gummy candies (cut in half)
- 24 Lifesavers candies
- 24 marshmallow peeps (Rabbit peeps)
- 24 Swiss rolls
- 48 M&M's plain chocolate candy
- 96 Spree candies

Directions:

1. Clean off a flat surface and unwrap all the Swiss cake rolls.
2. Scoop the frosting into a plastic zipper bag and pipe it into a corner.
3. Seal the bag and cut the corner.
4. Slice a V-shape into the bottom of the peeps, keeping it shallow. They should sit flat on the rolls.
5. Squeeze out a bit of frosting on the bottom of the peeps and stick them almost on the back of the cake rolls.
6. Use the frosting to attach the halved peach gummy slices to the back, which makes the back of the peeps' seat.
7. The Lifesavers are the steering wheels so attach them at an angle in front of the peep.
8. Use 2 matching M&M's as the headlights and attach to the front.
9. Use matching Spree candies or other candies if you prefer, and create tires, two on each side of the roll.
10. Finish the remaining rolls and enjoy!

46 - Bunny Bread

Ingredients:

Bread

- 1 teaspoon salt
- 1 tablespoon fast-rising active dry yeast
- ½ cup buttermilk, warmed
- ½ cup butter, room temperature
- ½ cup warm water (body temp)
- ½ cup sugar
- 5 cups all-purpose flour
- 2 eggs, beaten

Filling

- 1 teaspoon cinnamon
- ⅓ cup butter, room temperature
- ⅓ cup sugar
- ½ cup raisins
- ½ cup chocolate chips

Egg wash

- 1 egg, lightly mixed with water

Directions:

Dough Preparation

1. Use the directions on the bread machine to add the bread ingredients in the correct order as each machine is slightly different. Otherwise, place all bread ingredients in a mixing bowl, mix and knead.
2. Press the dough cycle and let it process for a few minutes.
3. Slowly add more water if it needs it.
4. Set the dough cycle and let it mix.

Filling

1. As the dough kneads, combine the butter and sugar and set it to the side.

2. In a separate bowl, add raisins, chips, and cinnamon.
3. Mix together and set it to the side as well.

Bread Preparation

1. When you see that the dough is ready, punch it down and pinch off 8 pieces of dough: 4 pieces the size of golf balls for the ears and feet, 2 pieces half the size of golf balls for the hands, and 2 pieces a quarter the size of golf balls for the cheeks.
2. Flatten each piece into a disk-like shape and set a bit of the butter mix topped with 1 chip and 1 raisin on each piece.
3. Carefully fold the sides over to enclose and make them ball shapes on all pieces except the ears.
4. Set these aside.
5. Now take out the rest of the dough and roll it on a floured surface and shape it into an 18 x 8-inch (45 x 20 cm) rectangle.
6. Smear the butter/sugar mix onto the dough and add the raisin/chip mix on top.
7. Fold over the long sides to create a wide roll.
8. Tuck the head edge down and bottom up.
9. Make the neck area a little lighter and make the head smaller than the body.
10. Once the body has been shaped, place it on a cookie sheet. Be sure you grease it first.
11. Set the ears where you like and pinch them in.
12. Set the cheeks next and use a bit of egg wash to make them stick better.
13. Do the same thing with the hands and feet, using the egg wash as an adhesive.
14. To make toes, use peanuts.
15. Finally, brush the whole bunny with egg wash and then set it to rise in a warm place. This should take about 30 minutes.
16. While it's rising, set the oven to 350°F (175°C).
17. Bake the bunny for 30 minutes.
18. You can reattach hands, feet, cheeks, and ears using decorating icing or toothpicks.

47 - Easter Egg Nests

Ingredients:

- ¼ teaspoon water
- 3 tablespoons butter or 3 tablespoons margarine
- ½ cup flaked coconut
- 4 cups miniature marshmallows
- 6 cups Rice Krispies
- 2-4 drops green food coloring
- Miniature marshmallow peeps
- Jelly beans
- Chocolate egg

Directions:

1. Combine water and green food coloring in a bowl.
2. Add the coconut and stir until the coconut is green.
3. Let it sit on a baking sheet until dry.
4. Get out a large saucepan and melt the butter.
5. Keep the heat low.
6. Add marshmallows and stir constantly. Note: Use fresh marshmallows for best results.
7. Once melted, take off the heat and add the cereal.
8. Mix it until the cereal is coated in marshmallow.
9. Get out 2½-inch (6.25 cm) muffin pans and spray them with cooking spray.
10. Pour the mixture into the cups and shape them.
11. Allow them to cool completely before removing them from the pans.
12. Now add the coconut, marshmallow peeps, jelly beans, or chocolate eggs.
13. At room temperature, these treats should be stored for no more than two days in an airtight container. If storing in the freezer, the unused cups can be kept in an air tight container lined with wax paper up to 6 weeks.

48 - Choco Krispie Easter Treats

Ingredients:

- ¼ teaspoon oil or ¼ teaspoon cooking spray
- 2 ounces (60 gm) crispy brown rice cereal (unsweetened like Rice Krispies)
- 3½ ounces (100 gm) dark chocolate
- Mini chocolate candy (like M&M's)
- Assorted cookie cutters

Directions:

1. Use olive oil or cooking spray to grease the cookie cutters so they don't stick.
2. Line a baking sheet with paper and set the cutters on it.
3. In a microwave or over a warm-water bath, melt the chocolate.
4. Add the rice cereal.
5. Spoon out the mixture into the cookie cutters and press down.
6. Add the candies for decoration if needed.
7. Let the chocolate harden.
8. Refrigerate if necessary.
9. Once hardened, remove the cookie cutters and enjoy.

49 - Chocolate Creamy Easter Eggs

Ingredients:

- 1 teaspoon salt
- 1 teaspoon vanilla
- 1½ teaspoons corn syrup
- ½ cup sweetened condensed milk
- ½ cup butter, softened
- 1 lb (450 gm) semisweet chocolate
- 6 to 7 cups sifted icing sugar
- Yellow food coloring
- 1 ounce paraffin wax (optional)

Directions:

1. Add milk, butter, corn syrup, salt, and vanilla to a large mixing bowl and mix well.
2. Slowly add the icing sugar in 3 or 4 batches.
3. Be sure to stir well after each batch.
4. Mix everything together then knead the dough with your hands, adding more icing sugar if necessary.
5. When the mixture can hold a shape and looks smooth, it's done.
6. Break apart a quarter of the mixture and add yellow food coloring to it. This will be the yolk. Break it down further into 10 or 15 smaller balls and set them all aside.
7. Return to the larger ball and divide it into 10 to 15 balls. In the palm of your hand, flatten them and set one of the yellow balls in the center. Manipulate the white batter to make an egg shape.
8. On a cookie sheet, layout the eggs and cover with plastic wrap. This will prevent them from drying out.
9. Let them chill in the refrigerator for 4 hours.
10. To prepare the dipping chocolate, combine the chocolate and paraffin in a bowl and put it over hot, but not boiling, water.
11. Once the eggs have firmed, dip them into the chocolate using a fondue fork if possible.

12. Cover the cookie sheet with wax or parchment paper and sent the eggs there.
13. Let them cool once more until the chocolate has hardened.
14. Decorate to your liking.

50 - Peeping S'mores

Ingredients:

- 1 package (11½ ounce or 320 gm) Hershey's milk chocolate chips
- 1 package (14½ ounce or 400 gm) honey maid graham crackers
- 3 packages (16 count each) marshmallow peeps

Directions:

1. Open and take out the peeps from the package.
2. Break all the graham crackers so there are 48 quarters.
3. Get out a cookie sheet and line it with wax paper to prevent sticking.
4. Set all the graham cracker pieces on the sheet.
5. Melt ¾ of the package of chocolate chips. Follow the directions on the package for best results.
6. Once melted, carefully dip each peep and coat it with chocolate.
7. Set it on a graham cracker piece.
8. As soon as all the peeps are done, set the baking sheet in the refrigerator and let them sit for at least 15 minutes or until the chocolate completely hardens.
9. As they're hardening, melt the remaining chocolate chips.
10. Once melted, pour it into a plastic bag with a seal.
11. Squeeze the chocolate into a bottom corner and cut the corner so you can properly drizzle the chocolate.
12. Decorate the peeps with melted chocolate before returning them once more to the refrigerator to re-harden.
13. Enjoy at room temperature or microwave for 8 to 10 seconds and serve warm.

51 - Bunny Cups

Ingredients:

- ¼ cup vanilla frosting
- 2 cups cold milk
- Licorice stick
- Red food coloring
- 1 package (3½ ounce or 98 gm) vanilla instant pudding mix
- 4 pink jelly beans or 4 red jelly beans
- 8 oval cream-filled sandwich cookies
- 8 jelly beans (blue, green...they're for the eyes so you'll need 2 of whatever colors you want)

Directions:

1. Add pudding mix and milk to a bowl and beat for two minutes.
2. Once smooth, pour the mix into 4 smaller bowls and set them in the refrigerator.
3. Next cut the licorice into whiskers by cutting them widthwise into fourths, then lengthwise into thirds.
4. Set them off to the side for now.
5. Add food coloring to the frosting so the color is more pink than red.
6. Smear the frosting on the tops of the cookies so it's just a half inch (1.25 cm) from the edge.
7. As you're getting ready to serve, put two cookies in each pudding bowl to make ears.
8. Now finish decorating with jelly beans for eyes and licorice for whiskers.

Thank You

If you liked the recipes, please take a moment to leave a review at your favorite retailer.

Other Books by Brianne Heaton

- 51 Dump Cake Recipes: Scrumptious Dump Cake Desserts To Satisfy Your Sweet Tooth

- 56 Breakfast Sandwich Recipes: Irresistible Sandwich Ideas to Kickstart Your Morning

- 50 Holiday Dessert Recipes: Delectable Dessert Ideas For The Christmas Holidays And Other Special Occasions

- 46 Sriracha Flavored Recipes: Delicious Sriracha Hot Sauce Cookbook For A Spicy Palate

Get the latest update on new releases from the author at:

https://www.brianneheaton.com/newsletter

About the Author – Brianne Heaton

Brianne Heaton started off collecting recipes that her family and friends enjoyed. After receiving many requests for copies of the recipes, she decided to share them by writing recipes books that everyone would appreciate.

Visit Brianne's website at:

https://www.brianneheaton.com/

Connect with Brianne Heaton

I really appreciate you reading my book! Here are my social media contact information:

Friend me on Facebook: https://www.facebook.com/BrianneHeatonRecipeBooks/

Follow me on Twitter: https://twitter.com/brianneheaton

Check me out on Goodreads: https://www.goodreads.com/author/show/8121938.Brianne_Heaton

Subscribe to my newsletter: https://www.brianneheaton.com/newsletter/

Visit my website: https://www.brianneheaton.com/

www.ingramcontent.com/pod-product-compliance
Lightning Source LLC
Chambersburg PA
CBHW062102290426
44110CB00022B/2687